Do not go gentle : poems on death /
    edited and with an introd. by
    William Packard. -- New York : St.
    Martin's Press, 1981.

ISBN 0-312...

1. Death--Poetry. 2. Poetry--Collected
works. I. Packard, William.

PN6110.D4D6   808.81'9354   [19]

                        Wa   80-27832

Do Not
Go Gentle

DO NOT GO GENTLE

POEMS ON DEATH

Edited by William Packard

Foreword by Richard Eberhart

ST. MARTIN'S PRESS   NEW YORK

LIBRARY OF CONGRESS CATALOGING IN PUBLICATION DATA:

Main entry under title:

Do not go gentle.

   1. Death—Poetry.   2. Poetry—Collections.
I. Packard, William.
PN6110.D4D6   808.81'.9354   80-27832
ISBN 0-312-21469-3

Design by A. Christopher Simon

Do Not
Go Gentle

Table of Contents

ix

Acknowledgments

The editor wishes to thank the authors, their publishers, and their representatives for their kind permission to reprint poems and translations and prose excerpts in this anthology of poetry about death, as follows:

"Fortune-tellers say I won't last long," "Never again, Orpheus," "Nothing but laughter," "Dead, they'll burn you up," from *The Greek Anthology*, translated by Kenneth Rexroth, copyright © 1962 by The University of Michigan Press, reprinted by permission of Kenneth Rexroth and The University of Michigan Press, Ann Arbor.

Selections from M. Antoninus, from *The Thoughts of the Emperor M. Aurelius Antoninus*, translated by George Long, copyright © 1927 by The Knickerbocker Press, New York.

Selections from *The Golden Sayings of Epictetus*, translated and arranged by Hastings Crossley, M.A., copyright 1935 by MacMillan and Company, Ltd., London.

Excerpt from Book Sixteen, *The Iliad* of Homer, translated by Robert Fitzgerald, copyright © 1979 by Doubleday and Co., Inc.

Excerpt from Book Eleven, *The Odyssey* of Homer, translated by Robert Fitzgerald, copyright © 1961 by Doubleday and Co., Inc.

Excerpt from the *Apology* of Plato, from *The Works of Plato*, translated by Benjamin Jowett, copyright © 1979 by Oxford University Press.

Psalms 23, 39, and 90, from the King James Version of the Holy Bible.

#3 of Catullus, translated by Margaret Ryan and Robert Winner, reprinted by permission of the translators.

Excerpts from Canto 1 and Canto 22 of the *Paradiso* of Dante, translated by John Ciardi, copyright © 1977 by W. W. Norton and Co., Inc.

"Lament for the Makirs" by William Dunbar, "The Conclusion" by Walter Raleigh, "A Dirge" and "Vanitas Vanitatum" by John Webster, "At the Round Earth's Imagined Corner" and "Death, Be Not Proud" by John

Foreword

If you are well and healthy, death seems a repellent or slightly repellent subject, not to be thought about, except occasionally. Strong undergraduates tend to think it will never happen to them. It is way off in the distance, out of focus. They have a future. Death has a past. It places the dead in a vast, unknown category and territory, or in the air we breathe if they are cremated.

Death may be the most important topic to think about because it is the one question which is unanswerable. What becomes of us when we die? Of course, we know literally what becomes or may become of the body. But this does not satisfy us. Death is total rejection of life. It is absolute, final, and endless. It seems unthinkable, unreasonable, yet everybody has to come to the elementary fact that we are destroyed as having been living, and now we all come to a state that is unknowable. Life ends in death, and we are powerless to change the fact. It comes down to a banal sentence!

Death is a final mystery. Birth is a mystery too—the deep question of why we were born and why we were born as we are, beyond the know physicality. Yet through millenia, death has begotten more and deeper poems than has birth. Since birth has a future, it does not invite the deep introspection of mankind as much as death, because in death there is no ongoing or growth, but unconsciousness, decay, or transformation to air by fire. Some see these as ongoing—death a part of life, part of a process. There are ancient Eastern ideas of the growth of the soul through myriad existences and changes through time, also the idea of timelessness. There are many religions and philosophies, and there is the great idea of Christ with the promise of immortality. But whatever we think or believe, the fact which all who are living face is that we do not know what happens to us when we die. Death is the most important subject in life because we cannot conquer it. We have to achieve what attitudes we can come by in making our response to an unanswerable problem. It does not accommodate us; we have to accommodate it.

There have been noble utterances about death by great poets. ("Come lovely and soothing death"; "Death, be not proud"; "I strove with none"; "O just, mighty and eloquent death" . . .) I have the notion that to write a strong death poem you would have to have full life in you, that to celebrate it you would have to be most lifelike, least deathlike, for if you were anywhere near death you would not have the force, strength, or control to make pronouncements on this subject which has always repelled and fascinated mankind.

RICHARD EBERHART

xv

Introduction

All of us are going to die, yet none of us has any idea what death itself is all about.

And we don't even know where to go to find out about death. We don't want to lie to ourselves and say we are going to live forever, and yet we don't want to go in for any foolish false assurances and superstitions about death. So perhaps the most we can do is try to find out what past poets and prophets and philosophers have had to say about death.

That's what this anthology of poetry and prose about death will try to present.

We might begin by looking at some of the last words of some of the greatest men and women who ever lived, to see what was going through their minds at the instant they entered into the experience of death. For example:

When Socrates felt the hemlock begin to freeze his curious queer limbs, he said, "Crito, I owe a cock to Asclepius; will you remember to pay the debt?" And then he died.

When Jesus had suffered the agony of the cross to the very end of his endurance, he let out a loud cry and he said: "It is finished." And then he died.

When George Washington felt the coming on of death, he said. "I die hard." And then he died.

When Tolstoy knew the end was near, he said: "I have loved many." And then he died.

1

When Henry David Thoreau sensed he was leaving this life, he said: "One world at a time." And then he died.

When Goethe knew he was dying, he cried out: "Light, more light!" And then he died.

When Gertrude Stein realized she was beginning to lose awareness, she said: "What is the answer? . . . Well then, what is the question?" And then she died.

These last words tell us a great deal about the people who spoke them, but they do not really tell us anything at all about the experience of death itself.

Well then, we could always go to a dictionary and see how it defines death. The *Oxford English Dictionary* describes being "dead" as:

1. *That has ceased to live; in that state in which the vital functions and powers have come to an end, and cannot be restored . . .*

2. *Bereft of sensation or vitality . . . Inanimate . . .*

But this doesn't tell us anything at all about what that inanimate state is like, once we pass over into the experience of death.

Well then, we could always go to all the major world languages and see what word each one uses to express the idea of death:

2

ENGLISH	DEATH
GERMAN	DER TOT
DUTCH	DER DOOD
FRENCH	MORTE
SPANISH	MUERTE
ITALIAN	MORTE
YUGOSLAVIAN	SMRT
JAPANESE	SHI

And we could go on and on and on, listing the word for death as it occurs in Russian, Chinese, Latin, Greek, and Egyptian— but this would tell us nothing at all about death itself. It would tell us only that all the major world civilizations have had a word for something that they did not in the least understand.

Well then, because death is such a very specific personal experience, perhaps we should shift over to the first person singular. Perhaps I ought to drop the mask of editorial detachment and try to describe my own earliest experiences with death. I remember, as a child, the very first encounter with a creature that was dead:

> *a small child sits*
> *beside an old dirt road*
> *watching a swarm of tiny lice*
> *burn away the body of a dead bird*
> *white specks darting*
>
> *in and out*

3

and how they feast upon
the moult of feathers there
eating away
the yellow shell of beak
and entering into
the hollow sockets
where the eyes once were

the child wonders
what are these lice
each tiny life
a light?
and are these things aware
of where they are
civilizing
in the open air?
soon they themselves
will be picked off
by living birds
or by quick flicking tongues
of lizards

from "Peaceable Kingdom," WILLIAM PACKARD

And I also remember as a child going to visit an aged relative, and when I went out there on the porch where she was lying on a bed, I saw her face was a mass of wrinkles, and I watched as her fingers fumbled on the covers to hand me a chalky piece of white candy. One week later I was told that she was dead.

But all these early memories don't help me to know what to expect about death, except that it is an irreversible fact of nature, and there is nothing that anyone can do about it.

We might just as well look at the clinical studies of death that take place in the intensive-care units, where terminal patients are put on support systems of intravenous feeding, vitamins, glucose, fats, and amino acids. Often comatose, these patients are unaware of where they are, as they subsist at minimal levels of existence. Or, if they are conscious, they will usually go through a series of predictable attitudes toward their terminal condition. Elizabeth Kubler-Ross, the Swiss psychiatrist who wrote *On Death and Dying*, lists five steps that usually take place in a terminal patient at the news of his or her impending death: first, denial; then, anger; then, bargaining; then, depression; and finally, acceptance.

We might also consider all the various theories and reports about "false death" that have been published in recent years. The "near-death" experience is reported by Kenneth Ring, author of *Life At Death: A Scientific Investigation of the Near-Death Experience*. Ring studied cases of 102 persons who came close to clinical death through illness, accident, or attempted suicide. Almost half these cases reported an out-of-body experience that was characterized by an eerie peace and calm, as if one were entering into a dark region where there was the presence of a benign voice. And we all know the reports of persons who have experienced "near-death" by drowning, who say their entire lives seemed to pass before their eyes during what seemed an eternity of suspended sensibility.

5

There are lots of other theories and reports about the experience of death. Reincarnationists have had their own exotic speculations about death as a necessary passage from one lifetime to another. The idea is as old as Plato, and it is best expressed by Wordsworth in his "Ode":

> *Our birth is but a sleep and a forgetting:*
> *The Soul that rises with us, our life's Star,*
> *Hath had elsewhere its setting,*
> *And cometh from afar:*
> *Not in entire forgetfulness,*
> *And not in utter nakedness,*
> *But trailing clouds of glory do we come*
> *From God, who is our home . . .*

from "Ode: Intimations of Immortality
From Recollections of Early Childhood,"
WILLIAM WORDSWORTH

And religionists have had their own special speculations about death. My own great-grandfather, Dwight L. Moody, conducted the Moody and Sankey Crusades in the nineteenth century, and he wrote this extraordinary statement about his own death:

Someday you will read in the papers that D. L. Moody of
East Northfield, is dead. Don't you believe a word of it!
At that moment I shall be more alive than I am now,
I shall have gone up higher, that is all; out of this old

*clay tenement into a house that is immortal—a body that
death cannot touch; that sin cannot taint; a body fashioned
like unto His glorious body.*

*I was born of the flesh in 1837. I was born of the Spirit
in 1856. That which is born of the flesh may die. That
which is born of the Spirit will live forever.*

And even atheists have had their own skeptical speculations
about death. They insist that death is nothing but a void, an
oblivion which is inconceivable to our minds. They say it is as
if suddenly the sun and stars descended to the center of de-
spair and disappeared, the ages of decay came to an end, and
our identity did not endure. They say death is irrevocably
real.

But all these theories and all these reports about death are
no more than that, merely speculations. And the fact is that
while we have a lot of high-sounding words in our language
like escatology (the science of final ends) and thanatology (the
science of death and dying), we still do not have the slightest
idea of what the experience of death is all about.

Heraclitus may have said it best almost 2500 years ago—
"There awaits men at death what they do not expect or
think."

All the various cultures and world religions have had to
accept death as an inextricable fact of our earthly existence.
The Buddha saw it as such in 528 B.C., when he sat under a
bodhi tree for forty-nine days and gained enlightenment: "De-
cay is inherent in all compound things; work out your salva-
tion with diligence." And in China, Chuang-tse, the disciple

7

of Lao-tse, said: "When we come, it is because we have the occasion to be born, and when we go, we simply follow the natural course." And Confucius said: "If you do not understand life, how can you understand death?"

In ancient Egypt there was an entire religion that was based on death, and it took the form of those colossal pyramids that served as tombs for all the various Pharaohs. Khufu's pyramid covers half a million square feet, and it contains two and one half million stone blocks, each one averaging a weight of two and one half tons. And inside the pyramids, the dead bodies of the Pharaohs lay in a state of mummification, which was an Egyptian art that is described in the *Mycerinus* of Herodotus:

First they draw out the brains through the nostrils with an iron hook, taking part of it out in this manner, the rest by the infusion of drugs. Then with a sharp stone they make an incision in the side, and take out the bowels; and having cleansed the abdomen and rinsed it with palm wine, they next sprinkle it with pounded perfume. Then, having filled the belly with pure myrrh, cassia and other perfumes, they sew it up again, and when they have done this they steep it in natron, leaving it under for seventy days; for a longer time than this it is not lawful to steep it. At the expiration of seventy days they wash the corpse, and wrap the whole body in bandages of waxen cloth, smearing it with gum, which the Egyptians commonly use instead of glue. After this the relations, having taken the body back again, make a wooden case, in the shape of a man, and having made it they enclose the body; and then, having fastened it up, they store it in a sepulchral chamber, setting it upright against the wall. In this manner they prepare the bodies that are embalmed in the most expensive way.

8

The Greeks saw death as a fact of life itself. In Book XI of the *Odyssey*, the living Odysseus goes down into the underworld where he can confront the shades of dead heroes and his own ancestors, so he can learn the truth about his own destiny. And Thucydides in his *History of the Peloponnesian War* gives an eyewitness account of the plague of 430 B.C.:

The most terrible thing of all was the despair into which people fell when they realized that they had caught the plague; for they would immediately adopt an attitude of utter hopelessness, and, by giving in in this way, would lose their powers of resistance. Terrible too, was the sight of people dying like sheep through having caught the disease as a result of nursing others. This indeed caused more deaths than anything else.

But perhaps the most terrible observation that Thucydides has to make about the plague is the following:

As for the gods, it seemed to be the same thing whether one worshipped them or not, when one saw the good and the bad dying indiscriminately.

Socrates in Plato's *Apology* makes one of the greatest statements ever recorded about death:

For the fear of death is indeed the pretence of wisdom, and not real wisdom, being a pretence of knowing the unknown; and no one knows whether death, which men in their fear apprehend to be the greatest evil, may not be the greatest good.

Socrates goes on to say that death may be one of two things: either it is a state of nothingness, or else it is a migration of the soul to another world; and in either case, he argues, there is reason to hope for the best. Socrates concludes:

Wherefore, O judges, be of good cheer about death, and know of a certainty, that no evil can befall a good man, either in this life or after death. He and his are not neglected by the gods . . .

The Old Testament Jews did not believe in an afterlife— Moses was more concerned with the reality of divine justice in this lifetime. Perhaps this was a reaction by the Jews against the death religion of the Egyptians; in any event, *Genesis* teaches that death is a curse that is laid on life as a punishment for transgressing the will of God. In *Job,* death is seen as a relief from the evils of this life, in 2:11:

Why died I not from the womb? Why did I not give up the ghost when I came out of the belly?

In the Psalms, death is a thing to be feared and dreaded, like the valley of the shadow of death. In Psalm 6:5, David sings:

For in death there is no remembrance of thee: in the grave who shall give thee thanks?

In Ecclesiastes, death is seen as an awareness of life's inevitable end, in 3:19:

... man dies as animals die ... as the one dieth, so dieth the others; yea, they have all one breath; so that a man hath no preeminence above a beast: for all is vanity.

In Isaiah, only God can survive death, in 40:8:

The grass withereth, the flower fadeth: but the word of our God shall stand for ever.

In the New Testament, Jesus is the first major Jewish prophet to declare that his kingdom is not of this world, that his father's house has many mansions, and that the kingdom of heaven is beyond mortality. The Rabbis and Sadducees did not believe in any life after death, and the Pharisees believed in a silly afterlife where they could sit and tote up all their good deeds. But Jesus offers a revolutionary new idea when he says in Matthew 5:12:

Rejoice and be exceeding glad; for great is your reward in heaven.

This new idea about death comes out of one of the most violent and death-ridden periods of human history. Before the birth of Jesus, Herod orders the Massacre of the Innocents; and after the crucifixion of Jesus, the Romans destroy the city of Jerusalem in 66–67 A.D., slaughtering every man and woman and child in it.

Still, the idea of an afterlife spread rapidly, first among the early Christians by Paul, when he writes in I Corinthians 15–21:

*For since by man came death, by man came also the resurrection of
the dead.*

And this new idea of an afterlife also spread rapidly among
the Jews themselves—by the time of Rabbi Akiba, 40-135
A.D., most Jews believed in a life after death, and by the time
of the Talmud in 189 A.D., Judaism itself affirmed the idea of
an afterlife.

By the time of medieval Christianity, the idea of an after-
life was so universally accepted that Dante could describe the
state of the soul after death in the *Commedia* with mathe-
matical accuracy, assigning each vice its appropriate punish-
ment and each virtue is exalted reward, whether in the
Inferno or in the *Purgatorio* or in the *Paradiso*, depending on
the precise dogmas of Catholicism. It is all a highly figurative
speculation about death.

But meanwhile, the reality of death was something quite
different for the fourteenth century. Hundreds of thousands
were dying of the Black Death, a vicious bubonic plague that
was carried across the continent by rats, and this disaster was
giving rise to much more earthly representations of death as a
grinning grim reaper, in prints like "The Triumph of Death"
and all the "Dance of Death" engravings. And the *Monastic
Diurnal* according to the Holy Rule of Saint Benedict set
down the last rites for the burial of the dead:

*I commend thee to Almighty God, dearest brother (sister), and com-
mit thee to him whose creature thou art; that when thou hast paid
the debt of all mankind by dying, thou mayest return to thy Maker,
who formed thee from the dust of the earth . . .*

The Renaissance reaches its full skepticism about death in the melancholy figure of Hamlet. The entire play is a collision between the structured medieval world view and an acid Renaissance skepticism, as in the opening scene where Gertrude says:

> Thou know'st, 'tis common; all that lives must die,
> Passing through nature to eternity.

And Hamlet replies sarcastically:

> Ay, madam, it is common.

And there is an echo of the medieval universe when the ghost of Hamlet's father hints at his wanderings through purgatory:

> My hour is almost come,
> When I to sulphurous and tormenting flames
> Must render up myself . . .
>
> I am thy father's spirit;
> Doom'd for a certain term to walk the night,
> And for the day confin'd to fast in fires,
> Till the foul crimes done in my days of nature
> Are burnt and purg'd away. But that I am forbid
> To tell the secrets of my prison-house,
> I could a tale unfold whose slightest word
> Would harrow up they soul, freeze thy young blood,
> Make thy two eyes, like stars, start from their spheres,
> Thy knotted and combined locks to part,

And each particular hair to stand on end,
Like quills upon the fretful porpentine:
But this eternal blazon must not be
To ears of flesh and blood . . .

The acid Renaissance skepticism returns to haunt Hamlet himself:

For in that sleep of death what dreams may come
When we have shuffled off this mortal coil,
Must give us pause . . .

. . . the dread of something after death,
The undiscovered country from whose bourn
No traveler returns, puzzles the will,
And makes us rather bear those ills we have
Than fly to others that we know not of . . .

This Renaissance skepticism about death is made superbly visual in the churchyard scene, where Hamlet holds a skull in his hand, tosses it about and mocks at it, until he is told the skull was once the king's jester, Yorick—and Hamlet stares down at the skull as if he is staring into the face of death itself, as he says:

Alas! poor Yorick. I knew him, Horatio; a fellow of infinite jest, of most excellent fancy; he hath borne me on his back a thousand times; and now, how abhorred in my imagination it is! My gorge rises at it. Here hung those lips that I

14

have kissed I know not how oft. Where be your gibes now?
your gambols? your songs? your flashes of merriment that
were wont to set the table on a roar? Not one now, to mock
your own grinning? quite chapfallen? Now get you to my
lady's chamber, and tell her, let her paint an inch thick, to
this favour she must come; make her laugh at that . . .

And then the dead body of the drowned Ophelia is carried onstage, and we feel the full horror of death in this pathetic suicide of a breathless mad victim of Renaissance court intrigue. The play ends with a final assertion of skepticism in Hamlet's own dying words:

The rest is silence.

This note of skepticism and resignation is echoed in all the other plays, most notably in *Macbeth:*

Duncan is in his grave:
After life's fitful fever, he sleeps well.

Renaissance skepticism gives way to a trust in the Enlightenment of the human mind when it is free of any overlay of superstition or foolish false assurance. John Donne lay in his own sepulcher so he could experience what the posture of eternal repose would feel like, and this is typical of the new scientific spirit. So, too, are Donne's words in *Devotions XVII* written in 1623, where he powerfully asserts the universality of death for all men:

15

No man is an island, entire of itself; every man is a piece of the continent, a part of the main; if a clod be washed away by the sea, Europe is the less, as well as if a promontory were, as well as if a manor of thy friends or of thine own were; any man's death diminishes me, because I am involved in mankind; and therefore never send to know for whom the bell tolls; it tolls for thee.

Blaise Pascal (1623–1662) also shows the scientific spirit in his *Pensées,* as he systematically explores the existential reality of death:

199   Let us imagine a number of men in chains and all condemned to death, where some are killed each day in the sight of the others, and those who remain see their own fate in that of their fellows and wait their turn, looking at each other sorrowfully and without hope. It is an image of the condition of men.

And in one of the great outcries of the human heart, Pascal writes:

206   Le silence éternel des ces espaces infinis m'effraie.
(The endless silence of these infinite spaces terrifies me.)

In our modern world, the scientific spirit still prevails—both Goethe and Freud insist on the utter unknowability of death:

GOETHE: *It is quite impossible for a thinking being to imagine a nonbeing, a cessation of thought and life. In this sense, everyone carries the proof of his own immortality within himself.*

FREUD: *Our own death is indeed unimaginable and whenever we make an attempt to imagine it we can perceive that we really survive as spectators. Hence the psychoanalytic school could venture the assertion that at bottom no one believes in his own death, or to put the same thing in another way, in the unconscious every one of us is convinced of his own immortality.*

But at this point we must suspend our inquiry into death. Because no matter how many general statements we may give, we must remind ourselves again and again and again that death is not a general problem at all, because it is altogether the most specific of personal experiences. So perhaps one way we can represent death adequately is to recreate the death scenes of certain extraordinary individuals, to see what may have been happening as these three men entered into the experience of death:

December 5, 1791—Wolfgang Amadeus Mozart's Die Zauberflöte was performed on September 30 and was an overwhelming success, but Mozart himself is debt-ridden and fears he may have been poisoned—he has overworked himself dreadfully and is suffering from kidney disease—sudden fits of vomiting; he is unable to move his swollen hands and feet—a priest is sent for, but the church is reluctant to attend Mozart because of his membership in the Freemasons—a dizziness, more nausea, then a continual sinking sensation—Mozart is thirty-six years old, has been writing music since the age of six, has completed forty-one symphonies, much church music, innumerable concerti, sonatas, operas, songs—more dizziness, now an endless sinking as Constanze leans forward towards the still-breathing figure—all is darkness now as the rest of his deathless

17

music is released into the silent Austrian air—Mozart's body will be taken away and buried in an unmarked grave in St. Marx cemetery—

March 27, 1827—Ludwig von Beethoven is unshaven and emaciated—visitors to his chambers have to write out their questions and answers on blank pads because Beethoven cannot hear their words— Franz Schubert had come to pay his respects and Beethoven had said: "That man has the divine spark!"—but it is an entirely different kind of spark that is igniting the night sky right now in sudden brilliant flashes of white lightning bolts, and there are massive loud climactic crashes of thunder overhead which Beethoven himself cannot hear—he is delirious now, he opens his eyes, he raises an arm, he shakes his fist against the storming night sky, and then he falls backward on his bed—his last words are: "I shall hear in heaven."—

September 23, 1939—Sigmund Freud is eighty years old, he is an exile from Nazi Vienna living now in London, and he has had cancer of the mouth for some sixteen years although he has steadfastly refused to take anything to relieve the great pain, not even an aspirin—he still insists on smoking his favorite cigars—necrosis of the tissue creates a foul odor that keeps even his pet dog on the other side of the room—Freud tells his interne: "Some kind of intervention that would cut short this cruel process would be very welcome." And so Schur gives Freud a hypodermic of two centigrams of morphine that sends Freud into a deep sleep, deeper even than those unconscious areas that he had been exploring through psychoanalysis for so long—the injection is repeated in twelve hours, Freud falls into a coma, he does not wake up again—

How should we feel about our own impending death?

Modern religion does not give us very much guidance. The *Christian Hymnal* is filled with a lot of euphemisms about how death is like the fading of the daylight, as:

18

Abide with me: fast falls the eventide;
The darkness deepens: lord, with me abide:
When other helpers fail, and comforts flee,
Help of the helpless, O abide with me. . .

* * * *

Day is dying in the west;
Heaven is touching earth with rest:
Wait and worship while the night
Sets her evening lamps alight
 Through all the sky . . .

* * * *

Now the day is over,
Night is drawing nigh,
Shadows of the evening
Steal across the sky . . .

Compared with these meek verses, one would much prefer
the manly heroism of Walt Whitman, that great pan figure
who gives us one of the most hopeful statements ever made
about death, in *Song of Myself*:

All goes onward and outwards, nothing collapses,
And to die is different from what anyone supposes, and
luckier . . .

Has anyone supposed it lucky to be born?
I hasten to inform him or her it is just as lucky to die, and I
know it . . .

19

And one cannot help admiring the plain courage and wis-
dom of Robert Louis Stevenson in his essay "Aes Triplex," in
which we are encouraged to meet death face to face:

*And, after all, what sorry and pitiful quibbling all this is! To forego
all the issues of living in a parlour with a regulated temperature—as
if that were not to die a hundred times over, and for ten years at a
stretch! As if that were not to die in one's own lifetime, and without
even the sad immunities of death! As if it were not to die, and yet be
the patient spectators of our own pitiable change! The Permanent
Possibility is preserved, but the sensations carefully held at arm's
length, as if one kept a photographic plate in a dark chamber. It is
better to lose health like a spendthrift than to waste it like a miser.
It is better to live and be done with it, than to die daily in the
sickroom. By all means begin your folio; even if the doctor does not
give you a year, even if he hesitates about a month, make one brave
push and see what can be accomplished in a week. It is not only in
finished undertakings that we ought to honour useful labour. A
spirit goes out of the man who means execution, which outlives the
most untimely ending. All who have meant good work with their
whole hearts, have done good work, although they may die before
they have the time to sign it. Every heart that has beat strong and
cheerfully has left a hopeful impulse behind it in the world, and
bettered the tradition of mankind. And even if death catch people,
like an open pitfall, and in mid-career, laying out vast projects, and
planning monstrous foundations, flushed with hope, and their
mouths full of boastful language, they should be at once tripped up
and silenced: is there not something brave and spirited in such a
termination? And does not life go down with a better grace, foaming
in full body over a precipice, than miserably straggling to an end in
sandy deltas? When the Greeks made their fine saying that those*

whom the gods love die young, I cannot help believing they had this sort of death also in their eye. For surely, at whatever age it overtake the man, this is to die young. Death has not been suffered to take so much as an illusion from his heart. In the hot-fit of life, a-tip-toe on the highest point of being, he passes at a bound on to the other side. The noise of the mallet and chisel is scarcely quenched, the trumpets are hardly done blowing, when, trailing with him clouds of glory, this happy-starred, full-blooded spirit shoots into the spiritual land.

And one has to be grateful to Robert Frost, for saying it all so simply:

> *There may be little or much beyond the grave,*
> *But the strong are saying nothing until they see.*

All around us on our earth, the plants and the animals are saying nothing—but they all seem to sense it when their time to die has come, and they go into themselves quite quietly as if they knew that something of considerable importance were about to take place. The elephant seeks out its secret resting place, the cat curls up in a comfortable corner, and the swan floats out alone in its serenity to sing its last, most lovely song. All of this is like the simple serenity of Pope John XXIII, who once said:

> *My bags are packed, and I am ready to go.*

WILLIAM PACKARD

21

From The Greek Anthology

Fortune-tellers say I won't last long;
It looks like it from the newspapers;
But there is better conversation
In Hell than in an insane nation;
And a galloping jug will get there
Quicker than these loud pedestrians,
Tumbling down hill witless in the dust.

ANTIPATROS

Never again, Orpheus
Will you lead the enchanted oaks,
Nor the rocks, nor the beasts
That are their own masters.
Never again will you sing to sleep
The roaring wind, nor the hail,
Nor the drifting snow, nor the boom
Of the sea wave.
You are dead now.
Led by your mother, Calliope,
The Muses shed many tears
Over you for a long time.
What good does it do us to mourn
For our sons when the immortal

22

Gods are powerless to save
Their own children from death?

ANTIPATROS

Nothing but laughter, nothing
But dust, nothing but nothing,
No reason why it happens.

GLYKON

Dead, they'll burn you up with electricity,
An interesting experience,
But quite briefly illuminating—
So pour the whiskey and kiss my wife or yours,
And I'll reciprocate. Stop fretting your brains.
In Hell the learned sit in long rows saying,
"Some A-s are not B-s, there exists a not B."
You'll have time to grow wise in their company.

MARKOS ARGENTARIOS

From Marcus Aurelius

III. 3.

Hippocrates, after curing many diseases, himself fell sick and died. The Chaldaei foretold the deaths of many, and then fate caught them too. Alexander, and Pompeius, and Caius Caesar, after so often completely destroying whole cities, and in battle cutting to pieces many ten thousands of cavalry and infantry, themselves too at last departed from life. Heraclitus, after so many speculations on the conflagration of the universe, was filled with water internally, and died smeared all over with mud. And lice destroyed Democritus, and other lice killed Socrates. What means all this? Thou hast embarked, thou hast made the voyage, thou art come to shore; get out. If indeed to another life, there is no want of gods, not even there. But if to a state without sensation, thou wilt cease to be held by pains and pleasures, and to be a slave to the vessel, which is as much inferior as that which serves it is superior: for the one is intelligence and deity; the other is earth and corruption.

IV. 50.

It is a vulgar, but still a useful help towards contempt of death, to pass in review those who have tenaciously stuck to life. What more then have they gained than those who have died early? Certainly they lie in their tombs somewhere at last, Cadicianus, Fabius, Julianus, Lepidus, or any one else like them, who have carried out many to be buried, and then were carried out themselves. Altogether the interval is small [between birth and death]; and consider with how much trouble, and in company with what sort of people, and in what a feeble body this interval is laboriously passed. Do not then consider life a thing of any value. For look to the immensity of time behind thee, and to the time which is before thee, another boundless space. In this infinity then what is the difference between him who lives three days and him who lives three generations?

VI. 28.

Death is a cessation of the impressions through the senses, and of the pulling of the strings which move the appetites, and of the discursive movements of the thoughts, and of the service to the flesh.

VII. 32.

About death: whether it is a dispersion, or a resolution into atoms, or annihilation, it is either extinction or change.

VIII. 58.

He who fears death either fears the loss of sensation or a different kind of sensation. But if thou shalt have no sensation, neither wilt thou feel any harm; and if thou shalt acquire another kind of sensation, thou wilt be a different kind of living being and thou wilt not cease to live.

IX. 3.

Do not despise death, but be well content with it, since this too is one of those things which nature wills. For such as it is

25

to be young and to grow old, and to increase and to reach maturity, and to have teeth and beard and gray hairs, and to beget, and to be pregnant and to bring forth, and all the other natural operations which the seasons of thy life bring, such also is dissolution. This, then, is man, to be neither careless nor impatient nor contemptuous with respect to death, but to wait for it as one of the operations of nature. As thou now waitest for the time when the child shall come out of thy wife's womb, so be ready for the time when thy soul shall fall out of this envelope. But if thou requirest also a vulgar kind of comfort which shall reach thy heart, thou wilt be made best reconciled to death by observing the objects from which thou art going to be removed, and the morals of those with whom thy soul will no longer be mingled. For it is no way right to be offended with men, but it is thy duty to care for them and to bear with them gently; and yet to remember that thy departure will be not from men who have the same principles as thyself. For this is the only thing, if there be any, which could draw us the contrary way and attach us to life, to be permitted to live with those who have the same principles as ourselves. But now thou seest how great is the trouble arising from the discordance of those who live together, so that thou mayst say, Come quick, O death, lest perchance I, too, should forget myself.

From Epictetus

Death? let it come when it will, whether it smite but a part
or the whole: Fly, you tell me—fly! But whither shall I fly?
Can any man cast me beyond the limits of the World? It may
not be! And whithersoever I go, there shall I still find Sun,
Moon, and Stars; there shall I find dreams, and omens, and
converse with the Gods!

To a good man there is no evil, either in life or death. And
if God supply not food, has He not, as a wise Commander,
sounded the signal for retreat and nothing more? I obey, I
follow—speaking good of my Commander, and praising His
acts. For at His good pleasure I came; and I depart when it
pleases Him; and while I was yet alive that was my work, to
sing praises unto God!

Remember that thou art an actor in a play, and of such sort
as the Author chooses, whether long or short. If it be his good
pleasure to assign thee the part of a beggar, a cripple, a ruler,
or a simple citizen, thine it is to play it fitly. For thy business
is to act the part assigned thee, well: to choose it, is another's.

Keep death and exile daily before thine eyes, with all else

that men deem terrible, but more especially Death. Then wilt thou never think a mean thought, nor covet anything beyond measure.

CLXIII

Piety towards the Gods, be sure, consists chiefly in thinking rightly concerning them—that they are, and that they govern the Universe with goodness and justice; and that thou thyself art appointed to obey them, and to submit under all circumstances that arise; acquiescing cheerfully in whatever may happen, sure that it is brought to pass and accomplished by the most Perfect Understanding. Thus thou wilt never find fault with the Gods, nor charge them with neglecting thee.

CLXXXIX

What wouldst thou be found doing when overtaken by Death? If I might choose, I would be found doing some deed of true humanity, of wide import, beneficent and noble. But if I may not be found engaged in aught so lofty, let me hope at least for this—what none may hinder, what is surely in my power—that I may be found raising up in myself that which had fallen; learning to deal more wisely with the things of sense; working out my own tranquillity, and thus rendering that which is its due to every relation of life. . . .

From The Iliad

BOOK SIXTEEN

Then Patroklos,
disabled by the god's blow and the spear wound,
moved back to save himself amid his men.
But Hektor, seeing that his brave adversary
tried to retire, hurt by the spear wound, charged
straight at him through the ranks and lunged for him
low in the flank, driving the spearhead through.
He crashed, and all Akhaian troops turned pale.
Think how a lion in his pride brings down
a tireless boar; magnificently they fight
on a mountain crest for a small gushing spring—
both in desire to drink—and by sheer power
the lion conquers the great panting boar:
that was the way the son of Priam, Hektor,
closed with Patroklos, son of Menoitios,
killer of many, and took his life away.

Then, glorying above him, he addressed him:
"Easy to guess, Patroklos, how you swore
to ravage Troy, to take the sweet daylight
of liberty from our women and to drag them
off in ships to your own land—you fool!
Between you and those women there is Hektor's
war team, thundering out to fight! My spear

has pride of place among the Trojan warriors,
keeping their evil hour at bay.
The kites will feed on you, here on this field.
Poor devil, what has that great prince Akhilleus
done for you? He must have told you often
as you were leaving and he stayed behind,
'Never come back to me, to the deep sea ships,
Patroklos, till you cut to rags
the bloody tunic on the chest of Hektor!'
That must have been the way he talked, and won
your mind to mindlessness."

                    In a low faint voice,
Patroklos, master of horse, you answered him:
"This is your hour to glory over me,
Hektor. The Lord Zeus and Apollo gave you
the upper hand and put me down with ease.
They stripped me of my arms. No one else did.
Say twenty men like you had come against me,
all would have died before my spear.
No, Leto's son and fatal destiny
have killed me; if we speak of men, Euphorbos.
You were in third place, only in at the death.
I'll tell you one thing more; take it to heart.
No long life is ahead for you. This day
your death stands near, and your immutable end,
at Prince Akhilleus' hands."

                    His own death
came on him as he spoke, and soul from body,

bemoaning severance from youth and manhood,
slipped to be wafted to the underworld.
Even in death Prince Hektor still addressed him:
"Why prophesy my sudden death, Patroklos?
Who knows? Akhilleus, son of bright-haired Thetis,
might be hit first; he might be killed by me."

At this he pulled his spearhead from the wound,
setting his heel upon him; then he pushed him
over on his back, clear of the spear,
and lifting it at once sought Automedon,
companion of the great runner Akhilleus,
longing to strike him. But the immortal horses,
gift of the gods to Peleus, bore him away.

31

From The Odyssey

BOOK ELEVEN

"Now the souls gathered, stirring out of Erebos,
brides and young men, and men grown old in pain,
and tender girls whose hearts were new to grief;
many were there, too, torn by brazen lanceheads,
battle-slain, bearing still their bloody gear.
From every side they came and sought the pit
with rustling cries; and I grew sick with fear.
But presently I gave command to my officers
to flay those sheep the bronze cut down and make
burnt offerings of flesh to the gods below—
to sovereign Death, to pale Persephone.
Meanwhile I crouched with my drawn sword to keep
the surging phantoms from the bloody pit
till I should know the presence of Teiresias.

"One shade came first—Elpenor, of our company,
who lay unburied still on the wide earth
as we had left him—dead in Kirke's hall,
untouched, unmourned, when other cares compelled us.
Now when I saw him there I wept for pity
and called out to him: 'How is this, Elpenor,
how could you journey to the western gloom
swifter afoot than I in the black lugger?'

"He sighed, and answered: 'Son of great Laertes,
Odysseus, master mariner and soldier,

32

bad luck shadowed me, and no kindly power;
ignoble death I drank with so much wine.
I slept on Kirke's roof, then could not see
the long steep backward ladder, coming down,
and fell that height. My neck bone, buckled under,
snapped, and my spirit found this well of dark.
Now hear the grace I pray for, in the name
of those back in the world, not here—your wife
and father, he who gave you bread in childhood,
and your own child, your only son, Telemakhos,
long ago left at home.

                " 'When you make sail
and put these lodgings of dim Death behind,
you will moor ship, I know, upon Aiaia Island;
there, O my lord, remember me, I pray;
do not abandon me unwept, unburied,
to tempt the gods' wrath, while you sail for home;
but fire my corpse and all the gear I had,
and build a cairn for me above the breakers—
an unknown sailor's mark for men to come.
Heap up the mound there, and implant upon it
the oar I pulled in life with my companions.'

"He ceased, and I replied: 'Unhappy spirit,
I promise you the barrow and the burial.' "

From Plato

Apology

Wherefore, O judges, be of good cheer about death, and know of a certainty, that no evil can happen to a good man, either in life or after death. He and his are not neglected by the gods; nor has my own approaching end happened by mere chance. But I see clearly that the time had arrived when it was better for me to die and be released from trouble; wherefore the oracle gave no sign. For which reason, also, I am not angry with my condemners, or with my accusers; they have done me no harm, although they did not mean to do me any good; and for this I may gently blame them.

Still I have a favour to ask of them. When my sons are grown up, I would ask you, O my friends, to punish them; and I would have you trouble them, as I have troubled you, if they seem to care about riches, or anything, more than about virtue; or if they pretend to be something when they are really nothing—then reprove them, as I have reproved you, for not caring about that for which they ought to care, and thinking that they are something when they are really nothing. And if you do this, both I and my sons will have received justice at your hands.

The hour of departure has arrived, and we go our ways—I to die, and you to live. Which is better God only knows.

From The Psalms of David

Psalm 23

The Lord is my shepherd; I shall not
want.
He maketh me to lie down in green
pastures: he leadeth me beside the still
waters.

He restoreth my soul: he leadeth me in the
paths of righteousness for his name's sake.
Yea, though I walk through the valley of
the shadow of death, I will fear no evil: for
thou art with me; thy rod and thy staff they
comfort me.
Thou preparest a table before me in the
presence of mine enemies: thou anointest
my head with oil; my cup runneth over.
Surely goodness and mercy shall follow
me all the days of my life: and I will dwell in
the house of the Lord for ever.

Psalm 39

I said, I will take heed to my ways, that
I sin not with my tongue: I will keep my

mouth with a bridle, while the wicked is
before me.

I was dumb with silence, I held my peace,
even from good; and my sorrow was stirred.

My heart was hot within me, while I was
musing the fire burned: then spake I with
my tongue.

Lord, make me to know mine end, and
the measure of my days, what it is; that I
may know how frail I am.

Behold, thou hast made my days as an
handbreadth; and mine age is as nothing
before thee: verily every man at his best
state is altogether vanity. Selah.

Surely every man walketh in a vain shew:
surely they are disquieted in vain: he
heapeth up riches, and knoweth not who
shall gather them.

And now, Lord, what wait I for? my hope
is in thee.

Deliver me from all my transgressions:
make me not the reproach of the foolish.

I was dumb, I opened not my mouth; be-
cause thou didst it.

Remove thy stroke away from me: I am
consumed by the blow of thine hand.

When thou with rebukes dost correct
man for iniquity, thou makest his beauty to
consume away like a moth: surely every
man is vanity. Selah.

Hear my prayer, O Lord, and give ear
unto my cry; hold not thy peace at my
tears: for I am a stranger with thee, and a
sojourner, as all my fathers were.

O spare me, that I may recover strength,
before I go hence, and be no more.

Psalm 90

Lord, thou hast been our dwelling place
 in all generations.

Before the mountains were brought forth,
or ever thou hadst formed the earth and the
world, even from everlasting to everlasting,
thou art God.

Thou turnest man to destruction; and
sayest, Return ye children of men.

For a thousand years in thy sight are but
as yesterday when it is past, and as a watch
in the night.

Thou carriest them away as with a flood;
they are as a sleep: in the morning they are
like grass which groweth up.

In the morning it flourisheth, and groweth
up; in the evening it is cut down, and withereth.

For we are consumed by thine anger, and
by thy wrath are we troubled.

Thou hast set our iniquities before thee,
our secret sins in the light of thy countenance.

For all our days are passed away in thy wrath: we spend our years as a tale that is told.

The days of our years are threescore years and ten; and if by reason of strength they be fourscore years, yet is their strength labour and sorrow; for it is soon cut off, and we fly away.

Who knoweth the power of thine anger? even according to thy fear, so is thy wrath.

So teach us to number our days, that we may apply our hearts unto wisdom.

Return, O Lord, how long? and let it repent thee concerning thy servants.

O satisfy us early with thy mercy; that we may rejoice and be glad all our days.

Make us glad according to the days wherein thou hast afflicted us, and the years wherein we have seen evil.

Let thy work appear unto thy servants, and thy glory unto their children.

And let the beauty of the Lord our God be upon us: and establish thou the work of our hands upon us; yea, the work of our hands establish thou it.

From the Book of Revelation

CHAPTER 20

And I saw an angel come down from heaven, having the key of the bottomless pit and a great chain in his hand.

And he laid hold on the dragon, that old serpent, which is the Devil, and Satan, and bound him a thousand years.

And cast him into the bottomless pit, and shut him up, and set a seal upon him, that he should deceive the nations no more, till the thousand years should be fulfilled: and after that he must be loosed a little season.

And I saw thrones, and they sat upon them, and judgment was given unto them: and I saw the souls of them that were beheaded for the witness of Jesus, and for the word of God, and which had not worshipped the beast, neither his image, neither had received his mark upon their foreheads, or in their hands; and they lived and reigned with Christ a thousand years.

But the rest of the dead lived not again until the thousand years were finished. This is the first resurrection.

Blessed and holy is he that hath part in the first resurrection: on such the second death hath no power, but they shall be priests of God and of Christ, and shall reign with him a thousand years.

And when the thousand years are expired, Satan shall be loosed out of his prison,

And shall go out to deceive the nations which are in the

four quarters of the earth, Gog and Magog, to gather them together to battle: the number of whom is as the sand of the sea.

And they went up on the breadth of the earth, and compassed the camp of the saints about, and the beloved city: and fire came down from God out of heaven, and devoured them.

And the devil that deceived them was cast into the lake of fire and brimstone, where the beast and the false prophet are, and shall be tormented day and night for ever and ever.

And I saw a great white throne, and him that sat on it, from whose face the earth and the heaven fled away; and there was found no place for them.

And I saw the dead, small and great, stand before God; and the books were opened: and another book was opened, which is the book of life: and the dead were judged out of those things which were written in the books, according to their works.

And the sea gave up the dead which were in it; and death and hell delivered up the dead which were in them: and they were judged every man according to their works.

And death and hell were cast into the lake of fire. This is the second death.

And whosoever was not found written in the book of life was cast into the lake of fire.

CHAPTER 21

And I saw a new heaven and a new earth: for the first heaven and the first earth were passed away; and there was no more sea.

And I John saw the holy city, new Jerusalem, coming down from God out of heaven, prepared as a bride adorned for her husband.

And I heard a great voice out of heaven saying, Behold, the tabernacle of God is with men, and he will dwell with them, and they shall be his people, and God himself shall be with them, and be their God.

And God shall wipe away all tears from their eyes; and there shall be no more death, neither sorrow, nor crying, neither shall there be any more pain: for the former things are passed away.

And he that sat upon the throne said, Behold, I make all things new. And he said unto me, Write: for these words are true and faithful.

And he said unto me, It is done. I am Alpha and Omega, the beginning and the end. I will give unto him that is a thirst of the fountain of the water of life freely.

He that overcometh shall inherit all things; and I will be his God, and he shall be my son.

But the fearful, and unbelieving, and the abominable, and murderers, and whoremongers, and sorcerers, and idolaters, and all liars, shall have their part in the lake which burneth with fire and brimstone: which is the second death.

From Catullus #3

Mourn, you Venuses and little Cupids,
and all men who love the most beautiful things.
My dear girl's sparrow is dead,
my dear girl's delectable sparrow
whom she loved more than her own two eyes,
whom she loved more dearly than her mother.
For he would hop around in her lap
leaping here and there and chirping
to his only mistress.
Now he travels through the paths of darkness
to that place from which no one ever returns.
But cursed and wicked are you, evil shadows,
hell gods, you who devour everything beautiful:
because you have stolen away the sparrow
that was beautiful to me.
O evil act! O miserable little sparrow!
For it is your fault my girl's eyes
are red with flowing tears.

Tr. Margaret Ryan and Robert Winner

From Dante

Paradiso

Dante states his supreme theme as Paradise itself and invokes the aid not only of the Muses but of Apollo. He and Beatrice are in the Earthly Paradise, the sun is at the vernal equinox, it is noon at Purgatory and midnight at Jerusalem when Dante sees Beatrice turn her eyes to stare straight into the sun and reflexively imitates her gesture. At once it is as if a second sun has been created, its light dazzling his senses, and Dante feels the ineffable change of his mortal soul into Godliness. These phenomena are more than his senses can grasp, and Beatrice must explain to him what he himself has not realized: that he and Beatrice are soaring toward the height of Heaven at an incalculable speed. Thus Dante climaxes the master metaphor in which purification is equated to weightlessness. Having purged all dross from his soul he mounts effortlessly, without even being aware of it at first, to his natural goal in the Godhead. So they pass through the Sphere of Fire, and so Dante first hears the music of the spheres.

FROM CANTO I

The glory of Him who moves all things rays forth
   through all the universe and is reflected
   from each thing in proportion to its worth.
I have been in that Heaven of His most light,

43

and what I saw those who descend from there
lack both the knowledge and the power to write.
For as our intellect draws near its goal
it opens to such depths of understanding
as memory cannot plumb within the soul.
Nevertheless, whatever portion time
still leaves me of the treasure of that Kingdom
shall now become the subject of my rhyme.
O good Apollo, for this last task, I pray
you make me such a vessel of your powers
as you deem worthy to be crowned with bay . . .

FROM CANTO 22

My sense reeled and, as a child in doubt
runs always to the one it trusts the most,
turned to my Guide, still shaken by that shout;
and she, like a mother, ever prompt to calm
her pale and breathless son with kindly words,
the sound of which is his accustomed balm,
said "Do you not know you are in the skies
of Heaven itself? that all is holy here?
that all things spring from love in Paradise?
Their one cry shakes your senses; you can now see
what would have happened to you had they sung
or had I smiled in my new ecstasy.
Had you understood the prayer within their cry
you would know now what vengeance they called down,
though you shall witness it before you die . . ."

44

Lament for the Makirs

I that in heill was and gladness
Am trublit now with great sickness
And feblit with infirmitie:—
    Timor Mortis conturbat me.

Our plesance here is all vain glory,
This fals world is but transitory,
The flesh is bruckle, the Feynd is slee:—
    Timor Mortis conturbat me.

The state of man does change and vary,
Now sound, now sick, now blyth, now sary,
Now dansand mirry, now like to dic:—
    Timor Mortis conturbat me.

No state in Erd here standis sicker;
As with the wynd wavis the wicker
So wannis this world's vanitie:—
    Timor Mortis conturbat me.

Unto the ded gois all Estatis,
Princis, Prelatis, and Potestatis,
Baith rich and poor of all degree:—
    Timor Mortis conturbat me.

He takis the knichtis in to the field
Enarmit under helm and scheild;
Victor he is at all mellie:—
    Timor Mortis conturbat me.

That strong unmerciful tyrand
Takis, on the motheris breast sowkand,
The babe full of benignitie:—
    Timor Mortis conturbat me.

He takis the campion in the stour,
The captain closit in the tour,
The lady in bour full of bewtie:—
    Timor Mortis conturbat me.

He spairis no lord for his piscence,
Na clerk for his intelligence;
His awful straik may no man flee:—
    Timor Mortis conturbat me.

Art-magicianis and astrologgis,
Rethoris, logicianis, and theologgis,
Them helpis no conclusionis slee:—
    Timor Mortis conturbat me.

In medecine the most practicianis,
Leechis, surrigianis, and physicianis,
Themself fra ded may not supplee:—
    Timor Mortis conturbat me.

I see that makaris amang the lave
Playis here their padyanis, syne goes to grave;
Sparit is nocht their facultie:—
    Timor Mortis conturbat me.

He has done petuously devour
The noble Chaucer, of makaris flour,

The Monk of Bury, and Gower, all three:—
    Timor Mortis conturbat me.

The good Sir Hew of Eglintoun,
Ettrick, Heriot, and Wintoun,
He has tane out of this cuntrie:—
    Timor Mortis conturbat me.

That scorpion fell has done infeck
Maister John Clerk, and James Afflek,
Fra ballat-making and tragedie:—
    Timor Mortis conturbat me.

Holland and Barbour he has berevit;
Alas! that he not with us levit
Sir Mungo Lockart of the Lee:—
    Timor Mortis conturbat me.

Clerk of Tranent eke he has tane,
That made the anteris of Gawaine;
Sir Gilbert Hay endit has he:—
    Timor Mortis conturbat me.

He has Blind Harry and Sandy Traill
Slain with his schour of mortal hail,
Quhilk Patrick Johnstoun might nought flee:—
    Timor Mortis conturbat me.

He has reft Merseir his endite,
That did in luve so lively write,
So short, so quick, of sentence hit:—
    Timor Mortis conturbat me.

47

He has tane Rowll of Aberdene,
And gentill Towll of Corsorphine;
Two better fallowis did no man see:—
Timor Mortis conturbat me.

In Dumfermline he has done roun
With Maister Robert Henrysoun;
Sir John the Ross enbrast has he:—
Timor Mortis conturbat me.

And he has now tane, last of a,
Good gentil Stobo and Quintin Shaw,
Of quhome all wichtis hes pitie:—
Timor Mortis conturbat me.

Good Maister Walter Kennedy
In point of Death lies verily;
Great ruth it were that so suld be:—
Timor Mortis conturbat me.

Sen he has all my brether tane,
He will naught let me live alane;
Of force, I man his next prey be:—
Timor Mortis conturbat me.

Since for the Death remeid is none,
Best is that we for Death dispone,
After our death that live may we:—
Timor Mortis conturbat me.

WILLIAM DUNBAR

The Conclusion

Even such is Time, that takes in trust
      Our youth, our joys, our all we have,
And pays us but with earth and dust;
      Who in the dark and silent grave,
When we have wander'd all our ways,
Shuts up the story of our days;
But from this earth, this grave, this dust,
My God shall raise me up, I trust.

SIR WALTER RALEIGH

49

From William Shakespeare

From The Tempest

Ariel: Full fathom five thy father lies:
        Of his bones are coral made:
    Those are pearls that were his eyes:
        Nothing of him that doth fade,
    But doth suffer a sea-change
    Into something rich and strange.
    Sea-nymphs hourly ring his knell:
                [*Burden:* ding-dong.]
    Hark! now I hear them,—ding-dong, bell.

From Twelfth Night

Clown: Come away, come away, death,
        And in said cypress let me be laid;
    Fly away, fly away, breath;
        I am slain by a fair cruel maid.
    My shroud of white, stuck all with yew,
        O! prepare it.
    My part of death, no one so true
        Did share it.

    Not a flower, not a flower sweet,
        On my black coffin let there be strown;

Not a friend, not a friend greet
   My poor corse, where my bones shall be thrown.
A thousand thousand sighs to save,
   Lay me, O! where
   Sad true lover never find my grave,
   To weep there.

From Cymbeline

Guiderius: Fear no more the heat o' the sun,
             Nor the furious winter's rages;
          Thou thy worldly task hast done,
             Home art gone, and ta'en thy wages;
          Golden lads and girls all must,
          As chimney-sweepers, come to dust.

Arviragus: Fear no more the frown o' the great,
             Thou art past the tyrant's stroke:
          Care no more to clothe and eat;
             To thee the reed is as the oak;
          The sceptre, learning, physic, must
             All follow this, and come to dust.

Guiderius: Fear no more the lightning-flash,
Arviragus: Nor the all-dreaded thunder-stone;
Guiderius: Fear not slander, censure rash;
Arviragus: Thou hast finish'd joy and moan:
Both: All lovers young, all lovers must
             Consign to thee, and come to dust.

Guiderius:	No exorciser harm thee!
Arviragus:	Nor no witchcraft charm thee!
Guiderius:	Ghost unlaid forbear thee!
Arviragus:	Nothing ill come near thee!
Both:	Quiet consummation have;
	And renowned be thy grave!

Sonnets

LXVI

Tir'd with all these, for restful death I cry
As to behold desert a beggar born,
And needy nothing trimm'd in jollity,
And purest faith unhappily forsworn,
And gilded honour shamefully misplac'd,
And maiden virtue rudely strumpeted,
And right perfection wrongfully disgraced,
And strength by limping sway disabled,
And art made tongue-tied by authority,
And folly—doctor-like—controlling skill,
And simple truth miscall'd simplicity,
And captive good attending captain ill:
 Tir'd with all these, from these would I be
  gone,
 Save that, to die, I leave my love alone.

LXXII

No longer mourn for me when I am dead

52

Than you shall hear the surly sullen bell
Give warning to the world that I am fled
From this vile world, with vilest worms to dwell:
Nay, if you read this line, remember not
The hand that writ it; for I love you so,
That I in your sweet thoughts would be forgot,
If thinking on me then should make you woe.
O! if,—I say, you look upon this verse,
When I perhaps compounded am with clay,
Do not so much as my poor name rehearse,
But let your love even with my life decay;
    Lest the wise world should look into your
      moan,
    And mock you with me after I am gone.

From Measure for Measure

Claudio: Ay, but to die, and go we know not
          where;
    To lie in cold obstruction and to rot;
    This sensible warm motion to become
    A kneaded clod; and the delighted spirit
    To bathe in fiery floods, or to reside
    In thrilling region of thick-ribbed ice;
    To be imprison'd in the viewless winds,
    And blown with restless violence round about
    The pendant world; or to be worse than worst
    Of those that lawless and incertain thoughts
    Imagine howling: 'tis too horrible!

The weariest and most loathed worldly life
That age, ache, penury and imprisonment
Can lay on nature is a paradise
To what we fear of death.

From Richard II

King Richard: No matter where. Of comfort no man speak:
Let's talk of graves, of worms, and epitaphs;
Make dust our paper, and with rainy eyes
Write sorrow on the bosom of the earth;
Let's choose executors and talk of wills:
And yet not so—for what can we bequeath
Save our deposed bodies to the ground?
Our lands, our lives, and all are
    Bolingbroke's,
And nothing can we call our own but death,
And that small model of the barren earth
Which serves as paste and cover to our
    bones.
For God's sake, let us sit upon the ground
And tell sad stories of the death of kings:
How some have been depos'd, some slain in
    war,
Some haunted by the ghosts they have
    depos'd,
Some poison'd by their wives, some sleeping
    kill'd:

All murder'd: for within the hollow crown
That rounds the mortal temples of a king
Keeps Death his court, and there the antick
    sits,
Scoffing his state and grinning at his pomp;
Allowing him a breath, a little scene,
To monarchize, be fear'd, and kill with
    looks,
Infusing him with self and vain conceit
As if this flesh which walls about our life
Were brass impregnable; and humour'd thus
Comes at the last, and with a little pin
Bores through his castle wall, and farewell
    king!
Cover your heads, and mock not flesh and
    blood
With solemn reverence: throw away respect,
Tradition, form and ceremonious duty,
For you have but mistook me all this while:
I live with bread like you, feel want,
Taste grief, need friends: subjected thus,
How can you say to me I am a king?

From Julius Caesar

Caesar: Cowards die many times before their deaths;
        The valiant never taste of death but once.
        Of all the wonders that I yet have heard,

It seems to me most strange that men should
    fear;
Seeing that death, a necessary end,
Will come when it will come.

From Hamlet

Hamlet: To be, or not to be: that is the question:
           Whether 'tis nobler in the mind to suffer
           The slings and arrows of outrageous fortune,
           Or to take arms against a sea of troubles,
           And by opposing end them? To die: to sleep;
           No more; and, by a sleep to say we end
           The heart-ache and the thousand natural
               shocks
           That flesh is heir to, 'tis a consummation
           Devoutly to be wish'd. To die, to sleep;
           To sleep: perchance to dream: ay, there's the
               rub;
           For in that sleep of death what dreams may
               come
           When we have shuffled off this mortal coil,
           Must give us pause. There's the respect
           That makes calamity of so long life;
           For who would bear the whips and scorns of
               time,
           The oppressor's wrong, the proud man's
               contumely,

The pangs of dispriz'd love, the law's delay,
The insolence of office, and the spurns
That patient merit of the unworthy takes,
When he himself might his quietus make
With a bare bodkin? who would fardels bear,
To grunt and sweat under a weary life,
But that the dread of something after death,
The undiscover'd country from whose bourn
No traveller returns, puzzles the will,
And makes us rather bear those ills we have
Than fly to others that we know not of?
Thus conscience does make cowards of us all;
And thus the native hue of resolution
Is sicklied o'er with the pale cast of thought,
And enterprises of great pith and moment
With this regard their currents turn awry,
And lose the name of action.

From Macbeth

Macbeth: To-morrow, and to-morrow, and to-morrow,
Creeps in this petty pace from day to day,
To the last syllable of recorded time;
And all our yesterdays have lighted fools
The way to dusty death. Out, out, brief
      candle!
Life's but a walking shadow, a poor player
That struts and frets his hour upon the stage,

57

And then is heard no more; it is a tale
Told by an idiot, full of sound and fury,
Signifying nothing.

The Shrouding of the Duchess of Malfi

HARK! now everything is still,
The screech-owl and the whistler shrill,
Call upon our dame aloud,
And bid her quickly don her shroud!
Much you had of land and rent;
Your length in clay's now competent:
A long war disturbed your mind;
Here your perfect peace is signed.
Of what is't fools make such vain keeping?
Sin their conception, their birth weeping,
Their life a general mist of error,
Their death a hideous storm of terror.
Strew your hair with powders sweet,
Don clean linen, bathe your feet,
And—the foul fiend more to check—
A crucifix let bless your neck:
'Tis now full tide 'tween night and day;
End your groan and come away.

JOHN WEBSTER

Vanitas Vanitatum

All the flowers of the spring
Meet to perfume our burying;
These have but their growing prime,
And man does flourish but his time:
Survey our progress from our birth—
We are set, we grow, we turn to earth.
Courts adieu, and all delights,
All bewitching appetites!
Sweetest breath and clearest eye
Like perfumes go out and die;
And consequently this is done
As shadows wait upon the sun.
Vain the ambition of kings
Who seek by trophies and dead things
To leave a living name behind,
And weave but nets to catch the wind.

JOHN WEBSTER

From Holy Sonnets

(ii)

At the round earth's imagined corners blow
    Your trumpets, angels, and arise, arise
    From death, you numberless infinities

59

Of souls, and to your scattered bodies go:
All whom the flood did, and fire shall o'erthrow,
　　All whom war, dearth, age, agues, tyrannies,
　　Despair, law, chance hath slain, and you whose eyes
Shall behold God, and never taste death's woe.
But let them sleep, Lord, and me mourn a space,
　　For if above all these my sins abound,
'Tis late to ask abundance of thy grace
　　When we are there. Here on this lowly ground
　　　Teach me how to repent: for that's as good
　　　As if thou hadst sealed my pardon with thy blood.

JOHN DONNE

(iii)

Death, be not proud, though some have called thee
　　Mighty and dreadful, for thou art not so;

　　For those whom thou think'st thou dost overthrow
Die not, poor Death, nor yet canst thou kill me.
From rest and sleep, which but thy pictures be,
　　Much pleasure—then, from thee much more must flow;
　　And soonst our best men with thee do go,
Rest of their bones and soul's delivery.
Thou'rt slave to fate, chance, kings and desperate men,
　　And dost with poison, war, and sickness dwell;
　　And poppy or charms can make us sleep as well,
And better than thy stroke. Why swell'st thou then?
　　One short sleep past, we wake eternally,
　　And death shall be no more. Death, thou shalt die.

JOHN DONNE

On my Son

Farewell, thou child of my right hand, and joy;
  My sin was too much hope of thee, loved boy.
Seven years thou wert lent to me, and I thee pay,
  Exacted by thy fate, on the just day.
O, could I lose all father now! For why
  Will man lament the state he should envy?
To have so soon 'scaped world's and flesh's rage,
  And, if no other misery, yet age?
Rest in soft peace, and, asked, say here doth lie
  Ben Jonson, his best piece of poetry.
For whose sake, henceforth, all his vows be such
  As what he loves may never like too much.

BEN JONSON

They Are All Gone into the World of Light!

They are all gone into the world of light!
  And I alone sit lingering here:
Their very memory is fair and bright,
  And my sad thoughts doth clear.

It glows and glitters in my cloudy breast
  Like stars upon some gloomy grove,
Or those faint beams in which this hill is dressed.
  After the sun's remove.

I see them walking in an air of glory,
  Whose light doth trample on my days:
My days, which are at best but dull and hoary,
  Mere glimmering and decays.

O holy Hope! and high Humility,
  High as the heavens above!
These are your walks, and you have showed them me,
  To kindle my cold love.

Dear beauteous Death! the jewel of the Just,
  Shining nowhere but in the dark;
What mysteries do lie beyond thy dust,
  Could man outlook that mark!

He that hath found some fledged bird's nest may know
  A first sight, if the bird be flown;
But what fair well or grove he sings in how,
  That is to him unknown.

And yet, as angels in some brighter dreams
  Call to the soul, when man doth sleep;
So some strange thoughts transcend our wonted themes,
  And into glory peep.

If a star were confined into a tomb,
  Her captive flames must needs burn there;
But when the hand that locked her up gives room,
  She'll shine through all the sphere.

O Father of eternal life, and all
  Created glories under thee!

Resume thy spirit from this world of thrall
    Into true liberty.

Either disperse these mists, which blot and fill
    My perspective still as they pass,
Or else remove me hence unto that hill,
    Where I shall need no glass.

HENRY VAUGHAN

When I Have Fears That I May Cease to Be

When I have fears that I may cease to be
Before my pen has glean'd my teeming brain,
Before high-piled books, in charact'ry,
Hold like rich garners the full-ripen'd grain;
When I behold, upon the night's starr'd face,
Huge cloudy symbols of a high romance,
And feel that I may never live to trace
Their shadows, with the magic hand of chance;
And when I feel, fair creature of an hour!
That I shall never look upon thee more,
Never have relish in the faery power
Of unreflecting love;—then on the shore
    Of the wide world I stand alone, and think,
    Till Love and Fame to nothingness do sink.

JOHN KEATS

The Dying Gladiator

I see before me the Gladiator lie:
    He leans upon his hand—his manly brow
    Consents to death, but conquers agony,
    And his drooped head sinks gradually low—
    And through his side the last drops, ebbing slow
    From the red gash, fall heavy, one by one,
    Like the first of a thunder-shower; and now
    The arena swims around him—he is gone,
Ere ceased the inhuman shout which hailed the wretch
      who won.

He heard it, but he heeded not—his eyes
    Were with his heart and that was far away;
    He recked not of the life he lost nor prize,
    But where his rude hut by the Danube lay,
    There were his young barbarians all at play,
    There was their Dacian mother—he, their sire,
    Butchered to make a Roman holiday—
    All this rushed with his blood—Shall he expire
And unavenged?—Arise! ye Goths, and glut your ire!

GEORGE LORD BYRON

Silence

There is a silence where hath been no sound,
    There is a silence where no sound may be,

In the cold grave—under the deep, deep sea,
Or in wide desert where no life is found,
Which hath been mute, and still must sleep profound;
    No voice is hushed—no life treads silently,
    But clouds and cloudy shadows wanter free,
That never spoke, over the idle ground:
But in green ruins, in the desolate walls,
    Of antique palaces, where Man hath been,
Though the dun fox, or wild hyena, calls,
    And owls, that flit continually between,
Shriek to the echo, and the low winds moan,
There the true Silence is, self-conscious and alone.

Thomas Hood

Prospice

Fear death?—to feel the fog in my throat,
    This mist in my face,
When the snows begin, and the blasts denote
    I am nearing the place,
The power of the night, the press of the storm
    The post of the foe;
Where he stands, the Arch Fear in a visible form,
    Yet the strong man must go:
For the journey is done and the summit attained,
    And the barriers fall,
Though a battle's to fight ere the guerdon be gained,
    The reward of it all.

I was ever a fighter, so—one fight more,
    The best and the last!
I would hate that death bandaged my eyes, and forbore,
    And bade me creep past.
No! Let me taste the whole of it, fare like my peers
    The heroes of old,
Bear the brunt, in a minute pay glad life's arrears
    Of pain, darkness and cold.
For sudden the worst turns the best to the brave,
    The black minute's at end,
And the elements' rage, the fiend-voices that rave,
    Shall dwindle, shall blend,
Shall change, shall become first a peace out of pain,
    Then a light, then thy breast,
O thou soul of my soul! I shall clasp thee again,
    And with God be the rest!

ROBERT BROWNING

Ozymandias

I met a traveller from an antique land
Who said: Two vast and trunkless legs of stone
Stand in the desert . . . Near them, on the sand,
Half sunk, a shattered visage lies, whose frown,
And wrinkled lip, and sneer of cold command,
Tell that its sculptor well those passions read
Which yet survive, stamped on these lifeless things,

66

The hand that mocked them, and the heart that fed:
And on the pedestal these words appear:
'My name is Ozymandias, king of kings:
Look on my works, ye Mighty, and despair!'
Nothing beside remains. Round the decay
Of that colossal wreck, boundless and bare
The lone and level sands stretch far away.

PERCY BYSSHE SHELLEY

Requiem

Under the wide and starry sky,
Dig the grave and let me lie.
Glad did I live and gladly die,
   And I laid me down with a will.

This be the verse you grave for me:
Here he lies where he longed to be;
Home is the sailor, home from sea,
   And the hunter home from the hill.

ROBERT LOUIS STEVENSON

Terminus

It is time to be old,
To take in sail:—

The god of bounds,
Who sets to seas a shore,
Came to me in his fatal rounds,
And said: 'No more!
No farther shoot
Thy broad ambitious branches, and thy root.
Fancy departs: no more invent;
Contract thy firmament
To compass of a tent.
There's not enough for this and that,
Make thy option which of two;
Economize the failing river,
Not the less revere the Giver,
Leave the many and hold the few.
Timely wise accept the terms,
Soften the fall with wary foot;
A little while
Still plan and smile,
And,—fault of novel germs,—
Mature the unfallen fruit.
Curse, if thou wilt, thy sires,
Bad husbands of their fires,
Who, when they gave thee breath,
Failed to bequeath
The needful sinew stark as once,
The Baresark marrow to thy bones,
But left a legacy of ebbing veins,
Inconstant heat and nerveless reins,—
Amid the Muses, left thee deaf and dumb,
Amid the gladiators, halt and numb.'

As the bird trims her to the gale,
I trim myself to the storm of time,
I man the rudder, reef the sail,
Obey the voice at eve obeyed at prime:
'Lowly faithful, banish fear,
Right onward drive unharmed;
The port, well worth the cruise, is near,
And every wave is charmed.'

RALPH WALDO EMERSON

The Soldier

If I should die, think only this of me:
  That there's some corner of a foreign field
That is for ever England. There shall be
  In that rich earth a richer dust concealed;
A dust whom England bore, shaped, made aware,
  Gave, once, her flowers to love, her ways to roam,
A body of England's, breathing English air,
  Washed by the rivers, blest by suns of home.

And think, this heart, all evil shed away,
  A pulse in the eternal mind, no less
    Gives somewhere back the thoughts by England given;
Her sights and sounds; dreams happy as her day;
  And laughter, learnt of friends; and gentleness,
    In hearts at peace, under an English heaven.

RUPERT BROOKE

From War and Peace

He dreamed that he was lying in the very room in which he was lying in reality, but that he was not ill, but quite well. Many people of various sorts, indifferent people of no importance, were present. He was talking and disputing with them about some trivial matter. They seemed to be preparing to set off somewhere. Prince Andrey had a dim feeling that all this was of no consequence, and that he had other matters of graver moment to think of, but still he went on uttering empty witticisms of some sort that surprised them. By degrees all these people began to disappear, and the one thing left was the question of closing the door. He got up and went towards the door to close it and bolt it. Everything depended on whether he were in time to shut it or not. He was going, he was hurrying, but his legs would not move, and he knew that he would not have time to shut the door, but still he was painfully straining every effort to do so. And an agonising terror came upon him. And that terror was the fear of death; behind the door stood It. But while he is helplessly and clumsily struggling towards the door, that something awful is already pressing against the other side of it, and forcing the door open. Something not human—death—is forcing the door open, and he must hold it to. He clutches at the door with a last straining effort—to shut it is impossible, at least to hold it—but his efforts are feeble and awkward; and, under the pressure of that awful thing, the door opens and shuts again.

LEO TOLSTOY

70

From Walt Whitman

6

A child said *What is the grass?* fetching it to me with full
    hands,
How could I answer the child? I do not know what it is
    any more than he.

I guess it must be the flag of my disposition, out of hopeful
    green stuff woven.

Or I guess it is the handkerchief of the Lord,
A scented gift and remembrancer designedly dropt,
Bearing the owner's name someway in the corners, that we
    may see and remark, and say *Whose?*

Or I guess the grass is itself a child, the produced babe of
    the vegetation.

Or I guess it is a uniform hieroglyphic,
And it means, Sprouting alike in broad zones and narrow
    zones,
Growing among black folks as among white,
Kanuck, Tuckahoe, Congressman, Cuff, I give them the
    same, I receive them the same.

And now it seems to be the beautiful uncut hair of graves.

Tenderly will I use you curling grass,
It may be you transpire from the breasts of young men,
It may be if I had known them I would have loved them,
It may be you are from old people, or from offspring
	taken soon out of their mothers' laps.

This grass is very dark to be from the white heads of old
	mothers,
Darker than the colourless beards of old men,
Dark to come from under the faint red roofs of mouths.

O I perceive after all so many uttering tongues,
And I perceive they do not come from the roofs of mouths
	for nothing.
I wish I could translate the hints about the dead young
	men and women,
And the hints about old men and mothers, and the offspring
	taken soon out of their laps.

What do you think has become of the young and old men?
And what do you think has become of the women and
	children?

They are alive and well somewhere,
The smallest sprout shows there is really no death,
And if ever there was it led forward life, and does not
	wait at the end to arrest it,
And ceas'd the moment life appear'd.

All goes onward and outward, nothing collapses,
And to die is different from what any one supposed, and
	luckier.

Has any one supposed it lucky to be born?
I hasten to inform him or her it is just as lucky to die,
      and I know it.

I pass death with the dying and birth with the new-wash'd
      babe, and am not contain'd between my hat and boots,
And peruse manifold objects, no two alike and every one
      good,

I am not an earth nor an adjunct of an earth,
I am the mate and companion of people, all just as immortal
      and fathomless as myself,
(They do not know how immortal, but I know.)

Every kind for itself and its own, for me mine male and
      female,
For me those that have been boys and that love women,
For me the man that is proud and feels how it stings to be
      slighted,
For me the sweet-heart and the old maid, for me mothers
      and the mothers of mothers,
For me lips that have smiled, eyes that have shed tears,
For me children and the begetters of children.

Undrape! you are not guilty to me, nor stale nor discarded,
I see through the broadcloth and gingham whether or no,
And am around, tenacious, acquisitive, tireless, and cannot
      be shaken away.

Out of the Cradle Endlessly Rocking

Out of the cradle endlessly rocking,
Out of the mocking-bird's throat, the musical shuttle,
Out of the Ninth-month midnight,
Over the sterile sands and the fields beyond, where the
    child leaving his bed wander'd alone, bareheaded,
    barefoot,
Down from the shower'd halo,
Up from the mystic play of shadows twining and twisting
    as if they were alive,
Out from the patches of briers and blackberries,
From the memories of the bird that chanted to me,
From your memories sad brother, from the fitful risings
    and fallings I heard,
From under that yellow half-moon late-risen and swollen
    as if with tears,
From those beginning notes of yearning and love there in
    the mist,
From the thousand responses of my heart never to cease,
From the myriad thence-arous'd words,
From the word stronger and more delicious than any,
From such as now they start the scene revisiting,
As a flock, twittering, rising, or overhead passing,
Borne hither, ere all eludes me, hurriedly,
A man, yet by these tears a little boy again,
Throwing myself on the sand, confronting the waves,
I, chanter of pains and joys, uniter of here and hereafter,
Taking all hints to use them, but swiftly leaping beyond
    them,

A reminiscence sing.
Once Paumanok,
When the lilac-scent was in the air and Fifth-month grass
    was growing,
Up this seashore in some briers,
Two feather'd guests from Alabama, two together,
And their nest, and four light-green eggs spotted with
    brown,
And every day the he-bird to and fro near at hand,
And every day the she-bird crouch'd on her nest, silent,
    with bright eyes,
And every day I, a curious boy, never too close, never
    disturbing them,
Cautiously peering, absorbing, translating.

Shine! shine! shine!
Pour down your warmth, great sun!
While we bask, we two together.
Two together!
Winds blow south, or winds blow north,
Day come white, or night come black,
Home, or rivers and mountains from home,
Singing all time, minding no time,
While we two keep together.

Till of a sudden,
May-be kill'd, unknown to her mate,
One forenoon the she-bird crouch'd not on the nest,
Nor return'd that afternoon, nor the next,
Nor ever appear'd again.

And thenceforward all summer in the sound of the sea,
And at night under the full of the moon in calmer
    weather,
Over the hoarse surging of the sea,
Or flitting from brier to brier by day,
I saw, I heard at intervals the remaining one, the he-bird,
The solitary guest from Alabama.

Blow! blow! blow!
Blow up sea-winds along Paumanok's shore;
I wait and I wait till you blow my mate to me.

Yes, when the stars glisten'd,
All night long on the prong of a moss-scallop'd stake,
Down almost amid the slapping waves,
Sat the lone singer wonderful causing tears.

He call'd on his mate,
He pour'd forth the meanings which I of all men know.

Yes my brother I know,
The rest might not, but I have treasur'd every note,
For more than once dimly down to the beach gliding,
Silent, avoiding the moonbeams, blending myself with the
    shadows,
Recalling now the obscure shapes, the echoes, the sounds
    and sights after their sorts,
The white arms out in the breakers tirelessly tossing,
I, with bare feet, a child, the wind wafting my hair,
Listen'd long and long.

Listen'd to keep, to sing, now translating the notes,

76

Following you my brother.

Soothe! soothe! soothe!
Close on its wave soothes the wave behind,
And again another behind embracing and lapping, every
    one close,
But my love soothes not me, not me.

Low hangs the moon it rose late,
It is lagging—O I think it is heavy with love, with love.

O madly the sea pushes upon the land,
With love, with love.

O night! do I not see my love fluttering out among the
    breakers?
What is that little black thing I see there in the white?

Loud! loud! loud!
Loud I call to you, my love!
High and clear I shoot my voice over the waves,
Surely you must know who is here, is here,
You must know who I am, my love.

Low-hanging moon!
What is that dusky spot in your brown yellow?
O it is the shape, the shape of my mate!
O moon do not keep her from me any longer.

Land! land! O land!
Whichever way I turn, O I think you could give me my
    mate back again if you only would,
For I am almost sure I see her dimly whichever way I look.

77

O rising stars!
Perhaps the one I want so much will rise, will rise with
some of you.

O throat! O trembling throat!
Sound clearer through the atmosphere!
Pierce the woods, the earth,
Somewhere listening to catch you must be the one I want.

Shake out carols!
Solitary here, the night's carols!
Carols of lonesome love! death's carols!
Carols under that lagging, yellow, waning moon!
O under that moon where she droops almost down into the
sea!
O reckless despairing carols.

But soft! sink low!
Soft! let me just murmur,
And do you wait a moment you husky-nois'd sea,
For somewhere I believe I heard my mate responding to
me,
So faint, I must be still, be still to listen,
But not altogether still, for then she might not come
immediately to me.

Hither my love!
Here I am! here!
With this just-sustain'd note I announce myself to you,
This gentle call is for you my love, for you.

Do not be decoy'd elsewhere,
That is the whistle of the wind, it is not my voice,
That is the fluttering, the fluttering of the spray,
Those are the shadows of leaves.

O darkness! O in vain!
O I am very sick and sorrowful.
O brown halo in the sky near the moon, drooping upon the
    sea!
O troubled reflection in the sea!
O throat! O throbbing heart!
And I singing uselessly, uselessly all the night.

O past! O happy life! O songs of joy!
In the air, in the woods, over fields,
Loved! loved! loved! loved! loved!
But my mate no more, no more with me!
We two together no more.

The aria sinking,
All else continuing, the stars shining,
The winds blowing, the notes of the bird continuous echoing,
With angry moans the fierce old mother incessantly moaning,
On the sands of Paumanok's shore gray and rustling,
The yellow half-moon enlarged, sagging down, drooping,
    the face of the sea almost touching,
The boy ecstatic, with his bare feet the waves, with his
    hair the atmosphere dallying,
The love in the heart long pent, now loose, now at last
    tumultuously bursting,

The aria's meaning, the ears, the soul, swiftly depositing,
The strange tears down the cheeks coursing,
The colloquy there, the trio, each uttering,
The undertone, the savage old mother incessantly crying,
To the boy's soul's questions sullenly timing, some drown'd
     secret hissing,
To the outsetting bard.

Demon or bird! (said the boy's soul,)
Is it indeed toward your mate you sing? or is it really to
     me?
for I, that was a child, my tongue's use sleeping, now I
     have heard you,
Now in a moment I know what I am for, I awake,
And already a thousand singers, a thousand songs, clearer,
     louder and more sorrowful than yours,
A thousand warbling echoes have started to life within me,
     never to die.
O you singer solitary, singing by yourself, projecting
     me,
O solitary me listening, never more shall I cease perpetuating
     you,
Never more shall I escape, never more the reverberations,
Never more the cries of unsatisfied love be absent from
     me,
Never again leave me to be the peaceful child I was before
     what there in the night,
By the sea under the yellow and sagging moon,
The messenger there arous'd, the fire, the sweet hell
     within,

The inknown want, the destiny of me.

O give me the clew! (it lurks in the night here somewhere,)
Of if I am to have so much, let me have more!

A word then, (for I will conquer it,)
The word final, superior to all,
Subtle, sent up—what is it?—I listen;
Are you whispering it, and have been all the time, you sea
    waves?
Is that it from your liquid rims and wet sands?

Whereto answering, the sea,
Delaying not, hurrying not,
Whisper'd me through the night, and very plainly before
    daybreak,
Lisp'd to me the low and delicious word death,
And again death, death, death, death,
Hissing melodious, neither like the bird nor like my
    arous'd child's heart,
But edging near as privately for me rustling at my feet,
Creeping thence steadily up to my ears and laving me
    softly all over,
Death, death, death, death, death.

Which I do not forget,
But fuse the song of my dusky demon and brother,
That he sang to me in the moonlight on Paumanok's gray
    beach,
With the thousand responsive songs at random,
My own songs awaked from that hour,
And with them the key, the word up from the waves,

The word of the sweetest song and all songs,
That strong and delicious word which, creeping to my feet,
(Or like some old crone rocking the cradle, swathed in
    sweet garments, bending aside,)
The sea whisper'd me.

From Emily Dickinson

'My life closed twice before its close'

My life closed twice before its close;
    It yet remains to see
If Immortality unveil
    A third event to me,

So huge, so hopeless to conceive,
    As these that twice befell.
Parting is all we know of heaven,
    And all we need of hell.

'I heard a fly buzz when I died'

I heard a fly buzz when I died;
The stillness in the room
Was like the stillness in the air
Between the heaves of storm.

The eyes around had wrung them dry,
And breaths were gathering firm
For that last onset, when the king
Be witnessed in the room.

I willed my keepsakes, signed away
What portion of me be

Assignable—and then it was
There interposed a fly,

With blue, uncertain, stumbling buzz,
Between the light and me;
And then the windows failed, and then
I could not see to see.

'I felt a funeral in my brain'

I felt a funeral in my brain,
   And mourners, to and fro,
Kept treading, treading, till it seemed
   That sense was breaking through.

And when they all were seated,
   A service like a drum
Kept beating, beating, till I thought
   My mind was going numb.

And then I heard them lift a box,
   And creak across my soul
With those same boots of lead, again.
   Then space began to toll
As all the heavens were a bell,
   And Being but an ear,
And I and silence some strange race,
   Wrecked, solitary, here.

'Ample make this bed'

Ample make this bed.
Make this bed with awe;
In it wait till judgment break
Excellent and fair.

Be its mattress straight,
Be its pillow round;
Let no sunrise' yellow noise
Interrupt this ground.

'Because I could not stop for Death'

Because I could not stop for Death,
He kindly stopped for me;
The carriage held but just ourselves
And Immortality.

We slowly drove, he knew no haste,
And I had put away
My labor, and my leisure too,
For his civility.

We passed the school where children played
At wrestling in a ring;
We passed the fields of gazing grain,
We passed the setting sun.

85

We paused before a house that seemed
A swelling of the ground;
The roof was scarcely visible,
The cornice but a mound.

Since then 'tis centuries; but each
Feels shorter than the day
I first surmised the horses' heads
Were toward eternity.

'I died for Beauty'

I died for Beauty—but was scarce
Adjusted in the Tomb
When One who died for Truth, was lain
In an adjoining Room—

He questioned softly "Why I failed"?
"For Beauty," I replied—
"And I—for Truth—Themself are One—
We Brethren, are," He said—

And so, as Kinsmen, met a Night—
We talked between the Rooms—
Untill the Moss had reached our lips—
And covered up—our names—

Anne Rutledge

Out of me unworthy and unknown
The vibrations of deathless music;
'With malice toward none, with charity for all.'
Out of me the forgiveness of millions toward millions,
And the beneficent face of a nation
Shining with justice and truth.
I am Anne Rutledge who sleep beneath these weeds,
Beloved in life of Abraham Lincoln,
Wedded to him, not through union,
But through separation.
Bloom forever, O Republic,
From the dust of my bosom!

EDGAR LEE MASTERS

Lucinda Matlock

I went to the dances at Chandlerville,
And played snap-out at Winchester.
One time we changed partners,
Driving home in the moonlight of middle June,
And then I found Davis.
We were married and lived together for seventy years,
Enjoying, working, raising the twelve children,
Eight of whom we lost

Ere I had reached the age of sixty.
I spun, I wove, I kept the house, I nursed the sick,
I made the garden, and for holiday
Rambled over the fields where sang the larks,
And by Spoon River gathering many a shell,
And many a flower and medicinal weed—
Shouting to the wooded hills, singing to the green valleys.
At ninety-six I had lived enough, that is all,
And passed to a sweet repose.
What is this I hear of sorrow and weariness,
Anger, discontent and drooping hopes?
Degenerate sons and daughters,
Life is too strong for you—
It takes life to love Life.

EDGAR LEE MASTERS

Death

He's dead

the dog won't have to
sleep on his potatoes
any more to keep them
from freezing

he's dead
the old bastard—
He's a bastard because

there's nothing
legitimate in him any
more
     he's dead

He's sick-dead

        he's

a godforsaken curio
without
any breath in it

He's nothing at all
     he's dead

Shrunken up to skin

    Put his head on
one chair and his
feet on another and
he'll lie there
like an acrobat—

Love's beaten. He
beat it. That's why
he's insufferable—

    because
he's there needing a
shave and making love
an inside howl
of anguish and defeat—

89

He's come out of the man
and he's let
the man go—
                    the liar

Dead
        his eyes
rolled up out of
the light—a mockery

                    which

    love cannot touch—

    just bury it
    and hide its face—
    for shame.

WILLIAM CARLOS WILLIAMS

And Death Shall Have No Dominion

And death shall have no dominion.
Dead men naked they shall be one
With the man in the wind and the west moon;
When their bones are picked clean and the clean bones gone,
They shall have stars at elbow and foot;
Though they go mad they shall be sane,
Though they sink through the sea they shall rise again;

Though lovers be lost love shall not;
And death shall have no dominion.

And death shall have no dominion.
Under the windings of the sea
They lying long shall not die windily;
Twisting on racks when sinews give way,
Strapped to a wheel, yet they shall not break;
Faith in their hands shall snap in two,
And the unicorn evils run them through;
Split all ends up they shan't crack;
And death shall have no dominion.

And death shall have no dominion.
No more may gulls cry at their ears
Or waves break out on the seashores;
Where blew a flower may a flower no more
Lift its head to the blows of the rain;
Though they be mad and dead as nails,
Heads of the characters hammer through daisies;
Break in the sun till the sun breaks down,
And death shall have no dominion.

A Refusal to Mourn the Death, by Fire,
of a Child in London

Never until the mankind making
Bird beast and flower

Fathering and all humbling darkness
Tells with silence the last light breaking
And the still hour
Is come of the sea tumbling in harness

And I must enter again the round
Zion of the water bead
And the synagogue of the ear of corn
Shall I let pray the shadow of a sound
Or sow my salt seed
In the least valley of sackcloth to mourn

The majesty and burning of the child's death.
I shall not murder
The mankind of her going with a grave truth
Nor blaspheme down the stations of the breath
With any further
Elegy of innocence and youth.

Deep with the first dead lies London's daughter,
Robed in the long friends,
The grains beyond age, the dark veins of her mother,
Secret by the unmourning water
Of the riding Thames.
After the first death, there is no other.

Do Not Go Gentle Into That Good Night

Do not go gentle into that good night,
Old age should burn and rave at close of day;

Rage, rage against the dying of the light.

Though wise men at their end know dark is right,
Because their words had forked no lightning they
Do not go gentle into that good night.

Good men, the last wave by, crying how bright
Their frail deeds might have danced in a green bay,
Rage, rage against the dying of the light.

Wild men who caught and sang the sun in flight,
And learn, too late, they grieved it on its way,
Do not go gentle into that good night.

Grave men, near death, who see with blinding sight
Blind eyes could blaze like meteors and be gay,
Rage, rage against the dying of the light.

And you, my father, there on the sad height,
Curse, bless me now with your fierce tears, I pray.
Do not go gentle into that good night.
Rage, rage against the dying of the light.

DYLAN THOMAS

Passer Mortuus Est

Death devours all lovely things:
Lesbia with her sparrow
Shares the darkness,—presently
Every bed is narrow.

Unremembered as old rain
  Dries the sheer libation;
And the little petulant hand
  Is an annotation.

After all, my erstwhile dear,
  My no longer cherished,
Need we say it was not love,
  Just because it perished?

EDNA ST. VINCENT MILLAY

Dirge Without Music

I am not resigned to the shutting away of loving hearts in
    the hard ground.
So it is, and so it will be, for so it has been, time out of
    mind:
Into the darkness they go, the wise and the lovely. Crowned
With lilies and with laurel they go; but I am not resigned.

Lovers and thinkers, into the earth with you.
Be one with the dull, the indiscriminate dust.
A fragment of what you felt, of what you knew,
A formula, a phrase remains,—but the best is lost.

The answers quick and keen, the honest look, the laughter,
    the love,—
They are gone. They are gone to feed the roses. Elegant and
    curled

Is the blossom. Fragrant is the blossom. I know. But I do
    not approve.
More precious was the light on your eyes than all the roses
    in the world.

Down, down, down into the darkness of the grave
Gently they go, the beautiful, the tender, the kind;
Quietly they go, the intelligent, the witty, the brave.
I know. But I do not approve. And I am not resigned.

EDNA ST. VINCENT MILLAY

Epistle to be Left in the Earth

. . . It is colder now,

                    there are many stars,

                                        we are drifting

North by the Great Bear,

                    the leaves are falling,

The water is stone in the scooped rocks,

                                        to southward

Red sun gray air:

                    the crows are
Slow on their crooked wings,

                            the jays have left us:
Long since we passed the flares of Orion
Each man believes in his heart he will die.

95

Many have written last thoughts and last letters.
None know if our deaths are now or forever:
None know if this wandering earth will be found.

We lie down and the snow covers our garments.
I pray you,
        you (if any open this writing)
Make in your mouths the words that were our names.
I will tell you all we have learned,
                          I will tell you everything:
The earth is round,
                there are springs under the orchards,
The loam cuts with a blunt knife,
                        beware of
Elms in thunder,
               the lights in the sky are stars—
We think they do not see,
                  we think also
The trees do not know nor the leaves of the grasses hear us:
The birds too are ignorant.
                  Do not listen.
Do not stand at dark in the open windows.
We before you have heard this:
                       they are voices:
They are not words at all but the wind rising.
Also none among us has seen God.
(. . . We have thought often
The flaws of sun in the late and driving weather
Pointed to one tree but it was not so.)

As for the nights I warn you the nights are dangerous:
The wind changes at night and the dreams come.
It is very cold,
              there are strange stars near Arcturus,
Voices are crying an unknown name in the sky.

ARCHIBALD MACLEISH

The Groundhog

In June, amid the golden fields,
I saw a groundhog lying dead.
Dead lay he; my senses shook,
And mind outshot our naked frailty.
There lowly in the vigorous summer
His form began its senseless change,
And made my senses waver dim
Seeing nature ferocious in him.
Inspecting close his maggots' might
And seething cauldron of his being,
Half with loathing, half with a strange love,
I poked him with an angry stick.
The fever arose, became a flame
And Vigour circumscribed the skies,
Immense energy in the sun,
And through my frame a sunless trembling.
My stick had done nor good nor harm.

97

Then stood I silent in the day
Watching the object, as before;
And kept my reverence for knowledge
Trying for control, to be still,
To quell the passion of the blood;
Until I had bent down on my knees
Praying for joy in the sight of decay.
And so I left; and I returned
In Autumn strict of eye, to see
The sap gone out of the groundhog,
But the bony sodden hulk remained.
But the year had lost its meaning,
And in intellectual chains
I lost both love and loathing,
Mured up in the wall of wisdom.
Another summer took the fields again
Massive and burning, full of life,
But when I chanced upon the spot
There was only a little hair left,
And bones bleaching in the sunlight
Beautiful as architecture;
I watched them like a geometer,
And cut a walking stick from a birch.
It has been three years, now.
There is no sign of the groundhog.
I stood there in the whirling summer,
My hand capped a withered heart,
And thought of China and of Greece,
Of Alexander in his tent;

Of Montaigne in his tower,
Of Saint Theresa in her wild lament.

RICHARD EBERHART

From Kaddish

V

Caw caw caw crows shriek in the white sun over grave stones
    in Long Island
Lord Lord Lord Naomi underneath this grass my halflife
    and my own as hers
caw caw my eye be buried in the same Ground where I stand
    in Angel
Lord Lord great Eye that stares on All and moves in a black
    cloud
caw caw strange cry of Beings flung up into sky over the waving
    trees
Lord Lord O Grinder of giant Beyonds my voice in a boundless
    field in Sheol
Caw caw the call of Time rent out of foot and wing an instant
    in the universe
Lord Lord an echo in the sky the wind through ragged leaves
    the roar of memory
caw caw all years my birth a dream caw caw New York the bus
    the broken shoe the vast highschool caw caw all Visions
    of the Lord

Lord Lord Lord caw caw caw Lord Lord Lord caw caw caw
    Lord

The Lute in the Attic

I call you
The apples are red again in Chandler's Valley
    redder for what happened there
And the ducks move like flocculent clocks
    round and round, and round
The seven fat ducks whose mouths
    were wet crimson once
        O William Brewster Hollins
        I call you back!
    Come you and stand here
By the fog-blunted house that is silent now
And watch these terrible ducks moving
    slowly round the rock of Santa Maura.

        Your father's gone daft, Willy.
        Did you know that?
And Isalina's flaxen hair is the color of the mud
    at the bottom of Rathbeggin Creek.
Her teeth are crooked and yellow,
        more like an old sickly dog's
    than a woman's—but her eyes
    still hold their light, people say.

100

(Though for me it's a very strange light, Willy.
I remember I saw a different thing there
    a few hours before it happened—
  and the two of you lying naked together
  under the apple trees.
For myself, to be truthful, her eyes have changed.
  They are not at all as they were then.)

  In his poor unease your father
Has come to love rather fearful things.
"Don't hurt my spider-ladies!" he screams,
When Beth or Danny go in to clean around him.
It would be better if he died, the town whispers.

Sam Hanner drowned two summers ago.
  Old Krairly wanted to carve
"Lived on strong drink, but his last was weak"
On the stone—the Fathers said no, of course.
There was talk that Sam watched you do it.
  Did you know that?

    As this comes in
  and so much hate will go anywhere
I call you back
To lie here in the rain and the dark beside the willows
Hearing the voices of lovers under the flowery hedge
    O William Brewster Hollins
I call you back!

Come you and lie here at the side of your brother . . .
  I can tell you exactly how many times
  these seven lean ducks have gone

101

fiercely round the rock of Santa Maura—
And show you worse things than your father sees
And show you things far worse than your father sees, Willy.

KENNETH PATCHEN

Blow Gabriel

Blow Gabriel!
Blow Gabriel!
Blow Gabriel!
Blow Gabriel!
Gonna walk and talk, tell it at the Judgment
Walk and talk, tell it at the Judgment, God
What you gonna do at the Judgment
What you gonna do at the Judgment
No need to run at the Judgment
No need to run at the Judgment, God
The sun'll start running at the Judgment
The sun'll start running at the Judgment, God
No use to run at the Judgment
No use to run at the Judgment
Blow Gabriel!
Blow Gabriel!
Blow Gabriel!

Blow Gabriel!
Blow Gabriel! at the Judgment, God

Blow Gabriel!
Blow Gabriel!
Oh the Big Book is open at the Judgment
The Big Book is open at the Judgment
   Said the moon is bleeding
   Moon is bleeding
   Rocks is melting
   Trees are bowing
   Seas are boiling
   Graves are busting
   What you gonna do—
   What you gonna do—
   What you gonna do—
   Oh sinner!

Gonna walk and talk, tell it—

   Gonna meet my father
   Gonna meet my father
   Oh Lord
   Oh my Lord
   Oh my Lord
   It's gonna be a time
   Gonna meet my brother
   Gonna meet my brother
   Gonna meet my father
   Gonna meet my father

BLIND GARY DAVIS

Someday I'll Be Dead

Someday I'll be dead
and all of you will mourn,
not because I'm dead
because another one of you is gone.

You'll be thinking of your turn
just around the bend
where bowed beneath your Maker's feet
you will meet your end.

Someday I'll be gone
and you will have my cares
like puppets on a string dancing
up on makeshift airs
you'll wonder when your turn will come.

We're quite a marionette
a show for all to see
and when I'm dead and gone
you'll remember me.

Not as one you loved or knew,
as one you needed to get
your performance through.

LEO CONNELLAN

104

On the Anniversary of My Dying

Reason me this, what of the energy
about the eye, light subtle wink of sight,
glass to the world, passage from the how to what,
now that this lout lies doubtless on this slab?

What of the thumping through the heart, reason
me this, what of the horses in the blood,
rain to the mind, drainage of the sewer parts,
now that he sleeping in the long goodbye?

Reason me madness to explain this plain,
to answer the crook of his lifeless brow—
O riddle me meaning to the dumb decease
and the coming of spring on his dirtbed.

WILLIAM PACKARD

tell us
what things die
    flies die
    dice die
    icicles die
    bicycles die
    tricycles die
    electric typewriters die
    grains of rice die
    rhinoceri die

tired old horses die
dykes die
eyelashes die
christs die
vice presidents die
childhood idols die
greedy egos mad for adulation die
long distance lovers die
elderly alligators die
venus flytraps die
reluctant virgins die
dried prunes die
highwire artists die
sly vicious statesmen die
right fielders die
black widow spiders die
pythons die
hyenas die
long island ladies die
psychiatrists die
bearded poetry teachers die
hotel clerks die
montreal sweethearts die
stationery store owners die
psychic midwives die
first grade teachers die
high school principals die
retired bus drivers die
delicatessan attendants die

acolytes die
FBI men die
tunnel tollbooth token takers die
selfish elf children die
prismatic impresarios die
life prisoners die
lonely old elephants die
dieticians die
associate editors die
tightassed intellectuals die
fine old eyes die
pine trees die
distant cousins die
venetian streetcleaners die
girls in black slacks die
rye fields die
left handed lovers die
chrysler plymouth dealers die
deep sea divers die
people who lease seaplanes die
violinists die
folk in kyoto die
italian dictators die
tribal chieftains die
governors of north dakota die
taoists die
silent film stars die
dodos die
prehistoric trees creatures die

disarming lions die
tiny lice die
women in state insane asylums die
Reichstag fires die
acrid odors die

WILLIAM PACKARD

On the Death of a Young Poet (for Adrian)

he was a young god dying in a
rosy vision
he was the god of chance, and
under all his innocence
was a ghastly schemer
water nymphs combed him
out of their sea green hair
the king of the deep cleansed him
from his yellow stare
the whole earth groaned
under his shortness of years
i knew him briefly, he
seemed a nice, gentle
young man

DONALD LEV